American Philanthropy: Is Soros A
Robber Barron Or A Philanthropist?

By

Dr Olga Magdalena Lazin

1

George Soros, founder of Open Society Fund in 1979, has succeeded to create a new bases for civil society in places ranging from Haiti to Romania and from China to India. Now Soros has expanded also to Guatemala.

Although I began my study of philanthropy with the idea of focusing my research on the history of the Soros Foundations, that idea took new form once I met with George Soros in 1996.

We have learned recently that George Soros, the financier, was right; markets unregulated will go array. Just look at the 2008 financial meltdown.

I am going to prove that Mr. Soros is a charitable 'robber baron", the type of whistleblower that we all need in order to keep the money "rolling" smoothly, and sound the alarm when currencies are overvalued:

"I give away millions of dollars because I care about the principles of Open Society, and I can afford it."

George Soros (1995)[1]

This book focuses on the rise and experience of the Open Society Foundation Network that merges the profit motive with the non-profit motive to develop locally and regionally responsible civil society through international networks of communication.

---

[1] Quoted in Harvey Shapiro, "Advocating an Open Society: An Interview with George Soros," <u>United Airlines Hemispheres Magazine</u>, March 1996, p. 15.

Let us not forget that it was profit making that led to the creation of major U.S. foundations, so much money having been "dubiously" accumulated by capital barons that, for the money to be "saved" in the family name, it had to be donated to tax exempt organizations such as the Rockefeller Foundation.

George Soros, founder of Open Society Fund, has tried to create a new bases for civil society in places ranging from Haiti to Romania, and from China to India.

Although I began my study of philanthropy with the idea of focusing my research on the history of the Soros Foundations, that idea took new form once I met with George Soros in 1996.

My preliminary thoughts were presented to Soros in 1995 in order to

obtain his initial reaction to my
hypothesis involving juxtaposition of:

1. the stated goals and
   achievements of the Soros
   Foundations (as summarized
   verbatim from foundation
   reports, newsletters, and
   Soros World Wide Web
   pages on the Internet, as I
   told him during our intense
   discussions of May 15, 1996,
   in New York City) with

2. my hypothesis that he has
   taken a risky approach to
   international philanthropy
   that is uncommon.

In that juxtaposition I suggested that
Soros, by himself, has sought to create
an open society in each country, thus

hoping that other U.S. and European foundations would follow him into East-Central Europe, but they did not do so.

Indeed, most other foundations have not followed Soros lead because, as he himself noted in my interview with him, he has neglected the legal structure that they demand to protect themselves against risk of losing their tax-free status in their home country.

Bureaucratically conservative foundations, especially those based in the USA, where the largest corpus of tax-free funds is domiciled, do not in the main take the risks of donating abroad because they fear becoming enmeshed in legal problems related to tax reporting in their home base of operations.

Soros indicated to me his concern that scholarly analysis focusing mainly on his risk-taking approach could backfire. He is concerned that, given the anti-foreign tenor of many congressional representatives, the U.S. Congress may look for opportunities to develop legislation that could inhibit the transfer of U.S. official and private foundations assistance funds from leaving the country.

Although in my view Soros is unduly worried about possible U.S. Congressional activity against foundations,[2] nevertheless, I here reorient my approach to focus on Soros as only one example of international philanthropy (here often used with a much larger connotation incorporating

---

[2]It is noteworthy that the U.S. Congress has not succumbed to the "simplifying" flat-tax approach that implicitly would perhaps make charitable donations irrelevant.

universities, NGOs and voluntary associations), thus also focusing my work on the rise of foundation activity such as that of the European Foundation Center and the Japan Foundation in an era when new trade and finance blocks are emerging as follows:

European Union,

Vísegrad,

NAFTA,

Mercosur,

Association of Caribbean States,

Central American Common Market,

G-3,

G-8,

Asia Pacific Economic Cooperation

My thesis is that if trade and finance must globalize to survive effectively, so must philanthropy operate in the international sphere. Soros' approach is only one of several which helps us to rethink the method of opening all societies to change and decentralized modernization. I have personally volunteered and dedicated 20 years of my life to a non-profit, and learn all the in-s and out-s of it after meeting Soros at his Open Society headquarters in New York.

Soros--The Philanthropist

Indeed, Soros had been interested since his period in England to foster the democratic values of "an open society," as defined by the philosopher Sir Karl Popper.[3] Determined to make Popper's

_____

[3] See Karl R., Popper The Open Society and Its Enemies, Princeton, New Jersey: Princeton University Press, 1995. Popper argues against the "closed

concept workable, Soros' Open Society
Fund became the basis for the Open
Society Fund, Inc. to which he has
donated so much of his dubiously-
earned profits to good ends.

Soros moved with high visibility into
philanthropy by establishing in 1984 the
Soros Foundation-Hungary and in 1987
the Soros Foundation-Soviet Union.
After the fall of the Berlin Wall in 1989,
Soros began to reposition himself by
turning over the day-to-day management
of his hedge fund to his staff so that he
could immerse himself in the world of
philanthropy. He was the only one who
recognized and was able to do
something about it that in those first
moments after 1989 liberation from
socialist dogma a new pattern of open

society" of unquestioned authority advocated by Plato
in The Republic.

society had to be set. His diagnosis was correct in that hardly had Russia and Eastern Europe overturned their dogmatic regimes that authoritarian forces attempted to seize power. This was hardly surprising because these had a complete absence of democratic experience and no modern political infrastructure was in place to support the new and fragile 'democracies.'

By 1990 he created three more foundations, moving into Central and Eastern Europe and the Soviet Union, dramatically accelerating the level of his giving. As Soros explains, "I have used financial markets as a laboratory for testing my theories... [on how to capitalize on] the collapse of the Soviet Empire."[4]

---

[4] <u>Soros on Soros</u>, p. v.

According to Soros' "Personal Statement" on the Soros Foundation World Wide Web Home Page, by early 1996 he was operating foundations in 24 countries. (The total is now 23, Belarus having this month withdrawn his legal recognition of Soros Foundation-Belarus, see below.)

Soros As Creator of Open Versus Closed Societies Via
The Network

To change the course of history and prevent the return of centralized authoritarian power in Eastern Europe, Soros has attempted to build the framework needed to support democracy. Thus, he has established a large number of independent branch foundations that offer services and vehicles of self-expression outside the reaches of an increasingly discredited state. Since governments have neither the will nor the resources to lead the kinds of initiatives they once though that they could lead, Soros has been the leader in arguing that the vacuum of leadership should be filled by a socially responsible private sector. Therefore, Soros has tried to set the philanthropic standard by opening branches of the Open Society Foundation around the globe.

Soros' views quoted below are taken from his oral interviews, speeches, books, articles, and foundation reports that provide the basis for his polyvalent concept 'open society,' as is seen for example in the 1994 Annual Report of the Soros Foundations:[5]

---

[5] P. 7.

The Soros is trying to make the family of Institutions independent by encouraging them to seek other sources of funding others than his own. As the Annual Report for the year 1994 puts it, "these organizations help build the infrastructure and institutions necessary for open societies by supporting a broad array of programs for education, children and youth, media and communications, civil society, human rights and humanitarian aid, science and medicine, arts, culture, and economic restructuring" Cit. Telecommunications and the Internet have been the main tools in Soros' hand in his crusade for establishing the pattern of open societies. His prominent

14

role in bringing down the Iron Curtain is indisputable.

The dramatic revolution and expansion in communications that took place during the 1980s, satellites, fax, copying machines, widespread dissemination of the computer opened the world's even most remote areas to the expanded communications links required for mass organization and concerted action contributed and accelerated the emergence of the fourth sector all around the world.

Analysis of Soros' use of the Internet shows how he uses electronic communication to influence other world leaders as well as how he uses the Net to unite the work worldwide of his foundations. Hence, he has initiated the Soros Foundation World Wide Web home page on the Internet.

George Soros has his own foreign policy. He has the money to back up his ideas and is spending it prodigiously. In 1994 alone, Soros' foundations around the world gave away $300 million, more than Portugal, New Zealand, or Ireland did, and he has spent a like amount in 1995. High-profile projects include a water purification plant in Sarajevo and a $500 stipend for each of 30,000 Russian scientists.[6] For the Soros actual expenditures for 1994, see Tables 1 and 2.

Since 1990 he has devoted half of his income and a substantially large portion of his time and energy to developing his foundation network.[7]

---

[6] Richard Teitelbaum, "What's Soros Up To Now?" Fortune, September 4, 1995,
   p. 94.

[7] Soros on Soros, p. 123.

In Soros' view, many Russians and Eastern Europeans are disillusioned and angry with the West, because the market economy being imported lacks a concept of common interest.[8] Soros agrees and notes that the U.S. model of untrammeled pursuit of self-interest does not represents the common interest. He argues that the U.S. model, which now dominates world development thinking, requires new rules and standards of behavior to circumscribe and contain competition, a measure of cooperation being needed to sustain competition.

The concept of open society is based on the recognition the world we live is inherently imperfect, as is human understanding of it, and although the

---

[8] George Soros, "Address to the [Central European University] Budapest Graduation Ceremony," CEU Gazette, Spring/Summer 1995, p. 15.

U.S. model is morally corrupt, the great merit of its open society is to permit correction of faults. For Soros, the Western democracies are morally bankrupt if they subsume common interest to the pursuit of narrow self-interest. [9]

Soros' goal is to turn the closed society of totalitarianism into an open society that follows Popper's prescription for setting "free the critical powers of man."[10] Before the revolutions that swept Central and Eastern Europe, dissidents had a similar goal; they called it "civil society," defined by some as" the connective tissue of democratic political culture." [11]

---

[9] Ibid.

[10] Popper The Open Society and Its Enemies, p.183.

[11] Soros "Address to the [Central European University] Budapest Graduation

Soros credits his membership in the Helsinki Watch and Americas Watch human rights groups as sparking him his 1980 creation Open Society Fund to offer a number of scholarships in the United States to dissident intellectuals from Eastern Europe.[12] To credit that spark, he recruited Aryen Neyer, who was the head of Human Rights Watch, to become the president of Soros' Open Society Institute in New York City.

With the human-rights orientation of spreading information, one of Soros' first projects had been to offer photocopying machines to cultural and scientific institutions, which was the perfect way to undermine the Communist Party control of information in Hungary. As copying

---

Ceremony," p. 15.

[12] Soros on Soros, p. 115.

machines increasingly became available in 1984, the Party apparatus could not control the machines and the dissemination of information, thus, as Soros has stated, his foundation in Hungary enabled people who were not dissidents to act, in effect, like dissidents. Similarly, the Soros grant program for writers increased their independence, therefore "disarming" the Party.[13]

Soros also tried to set up a foundation in China, establishing in 1986 the Fund for the Opening and Reform of China. That China operation was closed down by the Chinese government after the Tiananmen Square massacre, Soros being labeled as a "CIA agent."[14] Soros

[13] The view above and below is drawn from Soros on Soros, 118-123.

[14] Ibid., 139.

is optimistic about China, however, because with the rising number of fax machines and foreigners, it will be impossible to re-establish the rigid thought-control that prevailed previously.

To serve as "prototype" of open society, Soros' network of foundations has grown as follows: [15]

1984, Hungary

1986, China

1987, Russia

1988, Poland

1990, Bulgaria, Estonia, Lithuania, Romania, and Ukraine 1991, Yugoslavia

1992, Albania, Belarus, Bosnia & Hercegovina, Croatia,

---

[15] Soros Foundation, Internet Electronic Communications, World Wide Web, "National Foundations," WWW.Soros.Org, March 1996.

Czech Republic, Latvia, Macedonia, Moldova, Slovenia

1993, Kazakhstan, Kyrgyzstan, South Africa,

1994, Georgia

1995, Haiti, South Africa, Burma

1997, Guatemala

According to Soros, these national foundations are committed to certain common goals, such as the rule of a democratically elected government, a vigorous, diverse civil society, respect for minorities, and a free market economy. They also share a commitment to working together across national, ethnic, and religious boundaries to achieve these goals and such regional objectives as cooperation and peace among neighboring countries. The manner in which they pursue these goals is up to each national foundation, which, with its own staff and board, sets program priorities in response to the particular situation and problems in each country. These national foundations support, in part or in whole, a variety of internships abroad.

Recognizing the importance of incisive and responsible journalism, the Soros Foundations fund a broad array of activities to train and equip reporters, editors, and media managers for their new responsibilities in democratic, free market societies. The ultimate goal is to create an informed electorate that has access to diverse, objective are reports supplied by a press corps with high professional standards.

Foundations in Romania, Russia, and Ukraine have sent local journalists to CNN's U.S. headquarters in Atlanta,

Georgia, for the six-week International Professional Program. Foundations in the former Yugoslavia sent reporters to London for two months of training and work at the Balkan War Report, the highly regarded publication of the Institute for War and Peace Reporting. The Soros foundations' priorities in the area of communications are support for the establishment of strong, independent media as well as the expansion of telecommunications throughout the above-mentioned regions.

Censorship in Central and Eastern Europe and the former Soviet Union is now less explicit than it was under communist regimes, who required that all broadcasts and newspapers pass through an official censor. Governments, however, still control much of the physical infrastructure of media transmission therefore exercising indirect censorship.[16]

Promptly, the National Foundations provided the print media have received access to international news services, desktop publishing equipment, electronic mail, printing presses, and even newsprint.

News outlets supported by national foundations include

Radijocentras, Lithuania;

Radio Vitosha, Bulgaria;

Uniplus, Romania;

Radio Tallin, Estonia;

Radio Echo of Moscow, Russia;

Feral Tribune, Croatia;

Ieve magazine, Ukraine;

Pritonmost, Czech Republic;

Vreme, Yugoslavia.

---

[16] New York Times Editorial: "The Not-So-Free Eastern European Press," October 2, 1995.

In Russia, the foundation is providing funds to refurbish more than two dozen independent radio stations and to organize them into a network for sharing information.

Soros-funded programs in Romania and Macedonia have acquired second-hand printing presses in the United States. The presses were refurbished and placed in independent printing houses. In supporting democratic movements, often times Soros is accused of meddling in internal affairs. For example, in Romania when the Soros Foundations faced in 1991 the government's attempt to quash news by increasing prohibitively the price of newsprint at election time, the Foundation bought newsprint abroad and trucks to import paper so that independent newspapers could continue to publish. President Iliescu subsequently accused Soros of supporting the opposition, to which Soros responded that he was only supporting a pluralistic, free press. [17]

In Romania, Soros has administered since 1994 the first public surveys ever taken and published them as the "Public Opinion Barometer." The goal is to take the pulse of opinions about the country's economic and political life.

Soros is also founded in 1990 the Central European University (CEU) in Budapest, Prague, and Warsaw. The CEU is accredited in Hungary as degree-granting educational institution and prepares the leaders of the future. The CEU press publishing in English, Czech, Hungarian, Polish and Slovak

---

[17] Soros on Soros, p. 139.

languages provide news on the region in the domains of Literature, Political Science, Economics and European Studies.

Another fruitful program was established for the former Soviet and the Baltic states scientists, called the International Science Foundation. The scientists were given $100 million grant in order to continue their research in their native countries.[18] Emergency grants were given out of $500 to some 30,000 scientists, travel grants and scientific journals were provided, and the International Science Education Program is currently working to make the Internet available not only to the

_____

[18] This and the following discussion is based upon Building Open Societies: Soros   Foundations 1994, New York: OSI, 1994, pp. 15-35.

scientists but also to schools, universities, libraries and media.[19]

The Consortium for Academic Partnership, established in 1993, has expanded to include what Soros calls the "Virtual University," that is a program that includes:

CEU scholarships for students to pursue doctoral work in
the United States and Europe;
professorial exchanges for the CEU Economics School;
Freedom Support Act Fellowships;
supplementary grants for students from the former
Yugoslavia displaced by war;
supplementary grants for Burmese students.

---

[19] World Wide Web. Soros Or. The International Science Foundation.

Support of education, either directly or as a component of other programs, is the main focus of Soros foundations activity, amounting to about 50% of the expenditures, according to Soros sources.

Education based on the values of open, pluralistic, democratic societies proved to be the most effective way to break the grip of the communist past and prevent the emergence of new closed societies based on nationalism.[20]

One of the most comprehensive educational programs of the Soros Foundation are the Transformation of the Humanities Project and the Social Science Projects, which attempt to undo the previously state-controlled

[20] This information on education and the following comes from ibid. and Building Open Societies, pp. 15-19.

educational system in Russia and the other countries of the former Soviet Union and ex-satellite states. The ambitious project to replace Marxist-Leninist text books and teaching in school and universities has been undertaken in cooperation with the Ministry of Education and commissioned thousands of books, training professors, giving grants to innovative schools, introducing new curricula at selected demonstration sites in various disciplines.[21]

The new textbooks, as well as Western texts adapted and translated for Russia, are being published at a rate of ten a month and 10,000 copies a run. The Transformation of Humanities Project has been replicated in Ukraine,

---

[21] <u>Soros on Soros</u> , p.128.

Lithuania, Belarus, Estonia, Kazakhstan, Kyrgyzstan, Romania, Bosnia and Herzegovina, and Macedonia.

The Open Society Institute in Budapest conducts a number of research programs in collaboration with the CEU. Other foundations and programs created by George Soros include the International Science Foundation (ISF) and the International Soros Science Education Program, both of which encourage and support scientists and science teachers in the former Soviet Union so that they will remain at work in their home countries and not sell their skills to weapons producers in areas such as the Middle East.[22]

---

[22] These programs are discussed, e.g., in the Annual Report of the Soros Foundations, 1994, and summarized on the Soros World Wide Web Internet pages.

Russia has been a difficult country for Soros. He began organizing the Soviet Cultural Initiative Foundation in 1987 only to have the management of it fall into the hands of a reformist clique of Communist Youth League officials, who paradoxically proceeded to form a closed society to promote an open one.[23]

For Soros, Gorbachev had the great merit to have first shaken the rigid power structure and break the isolation into which the Soviet Union had fallen. Gorbachev thought of Europe as an open society, where frontiers lose their significance. He envisaged Europe as a network of connections, not as a geographic location, the network extending the concept of civil society through an international arena. Such

---

[23] Ibid., p. 128.

ideas could not be implemented by Gorbachev, but he must be credited with having planted them in infertile soil.[24]

In 1995, Soros reduced his financial investments in Russia, taking a "cautiously pessimistic' stance.[25] He is concerned that the xenophobic rhetoric by communists and nationalistic groups against greedy and exploitative foreigners is intended to provide an ideological justification for keeping the markets closed and protecting the resources for the state.[26] As Russia explodes out of the information vacuum

---

[24] George Soros, Opening the Soviet System (London, Weidenfeld and Nicolson, 1990), p. 102.

[25] Michael, Gordon R., "Cautiously Pessimistic," but Investing in Russia The New York Times,
        December 22, 1995.

[26] Michael, Gordon, R. "Russia's Woes Are Mirrored in the Decline of Coal Mines," New York Times, February 29, 1996.

that characterized the Communist era, the American magnate, financier-philanthropist is audaciously expanding access to the Internet and narrows the gap between Russia and the technologically advanced West.

Within his conception of open society, Soros sees the need for closer association between the nations of Europe, provided that the state not define or dominate the international activities of the citizenry. His concept holds great appeal for people who have been deprived of the benefits of an open society. [27]

Soros' priority is to help give access to the world of information not only to journalists, as we have seen, but to other professional groups, especially

[27] Soros, "Address to the [Central European University] Budapest Graduation Ceremony," p. 15.

including librarians and scientists as well as individual citizens. For Soros it is Electronic mail and Internet connectivity that hold the possibility of bringing to East-Central Europe and Russia a new method of communications particularly suitable to the building of open societies.[28]

Making telecommunications widely available promotes pluralism and undermines government attempts to control information (Belarus has recently shut down the Open Society Foundation exactly for this reason). The Open Society foundations are building telecommunications networks by providing computers, software, training and the Internet access to media centers, libraries, legal institutes, research laboratories, high schools,

[28] Open Society News, Fall 94, Electronic Edition, Soros Foundation (WWW.Soros.Org).

universities as well as Soros foundation offices. Information servers are also being designed at a number of Soros organizations.

The hub of the Soros Foundations' communications activities is Open Media Research Institute, a new research center established to analyze and report on the political, economic, and social changes under way in Central and Eastern Europe and the former Soviet Union. It is developing a media studies program to teach journalists, analysts, policy specialists, and scholars about the role of investigative journalism as well as the business of media.[29]

What Soros desires, it would seem, is not only an open society, which might be an ideal one, but the creation of civic society--what the Romans called *civitas;*

[29] Idem, click on CEENet.Internet.

that is, public-spiritedness, sacrifice for the community, citizenship, especially elites. It involves the creation of what Francis Fukuyama calls "trust."[30]

In his oral interviews, Soros admits how difficult it is running a foundation in a revolutionary environment of Russia and the Eastern European countries. Despite a bitter 1994 experience of attempting to operate a foundation at the height of Russia's period of "robber-capitalists," Soros sees his Transformation of the Humanities Project as very successful.[31]

To provide students with information on educational opportunities in the West, 23 Soros Student Advising

---

[30] Francis, Fukuyama, Trust: Social Virtues and the Creation of Prosperity, (New York: The Free Press, 1995), p. 27.

[31] Soros on Soros, passim, esp. p. 129.

Centers have been established in major cities in the Eastern European region. The foundations also promote the English language through a variety of local projects.[32]

Responding to the unique intellectual and emotional needs of children and teens, the Open Society Institute has initiated a series of regional programs to provide opportunities for the young people in the region and especially in the countries of former Yugoslavia.

At the time when a changing political landscape offers little stability, the Regional High School Debate Program and the Preschool Project promote independence and self-esteem,

---

[32] International Guide to Funders Interested in Central and Eastern Europe Central European Foundation Center (EFC), Brussels, Belgium, 1993, p.   147.

and encourage young people to take an active and critical role in their education.[33] Most national foundations contribute project support to indigenous, independent organizations which address cultural, major health or environmental problems in direct and practical ways: fellowships sending American volunteers abroad to teach environmental topics, donating medical supplies, distribution networks, and dollar conversion for the purchase of desired medical equipment.[34]

With regard to philanthropy for medical goals, Soros' concern about the problem in the USA caused him to

---

[33] Chris, Sulavek, "Empowering the Programs for Children and Teens,"
     Open Society News, Winter 1995, p. 5.

[34] International Guide to Funders Interested in Central and Eastern Europe, p. 147.

initiate a "Project on Death and Dying," dedicated to research and issues of terminal illness and pain management, on which he intends to focus more of his energies and funds. The goal of the Soros Project on Death in America is to help expand our understanding of and to transform the forces that have created and sustain the current culture of dying. The $5,000 million project supports epidemiological, ethnographic, and historical research and other programs that illuminate the social and medical context of dying and grieving.[35] In Soros' own words the American medical culture, "modern medicine is so intent on prolonging life that it fails to prepare us for death." The results of the research will help to encourage family

---

[35] George, Soros "Reflections on Death in America," Open Society News, Winter 1995, p. 2.

involvement and to reduce the dehumanizing effect of medical treatment. Under the Grants Program, Joseph's House in Washington, DC, a Project on Death on America grantee, provides a life-affirming community for people with AIDS.

Soros' foundations herald an era in which social and cultural responsibility, assumed by government up to the 1980s in Eastern Europe, is defined by private giving. Soros Foundation grants to Eastern Europe outstrip the amounts given by most Western corporate foundations in Europe. Soros' funding has gone less to construct capitalism than to rediscover the human riches of intellect that communism plundered.

In its focus on finance and government, the West has neglected the softer and subtler sides of free societies, and Soros' new Marshal plan (1989) was "greeted with amusement" by the Europeans. [36]

With regard to failure of policies he has supported, Soros notes with regret that the Russian programs partially failed because of his leaders there bought autos for their personal use. Therefore, he temporarily closed operations in order to organize an entirely new staff. The foundations involved in structural reforms in Ukraine, and Macedonia, the last surviving multi-ethnic democracy have been successful. The $50 million granted to the young Macedonian state just saved it from bankruptcy. (L'Evenement, No. 583, p.27)

---

[36] Barry, Newman, "Soros Gives to Help East Europe Recover Lost Cultural Treasures," New York Times, March 22, 1994.

In late February the Milosevic regime in Belgrade (Serbia) dealt a financial blow to Soros programs in two ways. It hurt all independent media by revoking the registration of the Soros Foundation, forcing it to close down operations in Serbia and Montenegro. This also has slowed the work of the Open Society Institute work in Belgrade where it is developing an important part of its A Balkan War Crimes Database.[37]

The Soros Foundation Model Unfollowed

Why has Soros won neither foundations or multilateral agencies to "invest" as he has in the development of post-communist society?

The answer has several parts. First, Soros has been concerned that his

---

[37] New York Times Editorial: "Censorship in the Balkans," March, 14, 1996.

Foundations not become the kind of bureaucratic operation run by a meritocratic elite for itself (thus requiring long lead time to develop projects) that has taken power in most foundations and all multilateral development banks and agencies. Second, as a consequence of the first point, Soros has been able to do what most foundations cannot do not only because his entire financial trading history is based upon that of being a risk-taker who grasps the moment. Because most foundation leaders and all leaders of multilateral development and banking agency are risk averse, too often they miss the opportunity to be a part of genuinely new programs.   To make grants without incurring total accounting responsibility over expenditures by the grantee, U.S. and U.S.-based multilateral banks and agencies must make pay their lawyers to make a legal determination that each grantee is the "equivalent to a U.S. NPPO" and if it would be eligible for certification by the IRS if it were a U.S. NPPO.

Soros' solution to the above legal problem is to have set up his own network of foundations that at once facilitates his grant making activity and gives them some independence, yet allows him to provide a check on expenditure should he not make new grants.

What happens when Soros runs out of money and/or dies? What has he institutionalized? The answers do not bode well for the future of the NPPO sector for which he hopes his foundations are the model for others to follow:

The problem is that without a NPPO legal framework to encourage Internationally-oriented foundation "investment" in Eastern Europe, the Soros Foundation Model cannot easily be followed, leaving Soros to stand alone as the funder of only resort. The challenge to Soros is not to be the sole funder in each country because the task of establishing the open basis for civil society requires the spending of billions of dollars by funders making the thousands of decisions no one organization can make. Beyond Soros' use of funds to support debate and spread of information, Soros must now help support the NPPO legal basis for the establishment of competing foundations. Without competition, Soros Foundation decisions about whom to fund have the political consequence of alienating those who are not funded and who are without other recourse as the State contracts.

Yet Soros' Open Society Institute, which itself is funded from the USA, determined at a 1995 meeting of the East Program, that "international funding is not the solution for the long-term future" of the NPPO sector in Russia and Eastern Europe. Hence, the meeting concluded that it should look inward to develop private funding sources in each country of the region.[38]

The East meeting not only runs counter to Soros' own experience of encouraging the flow of NPPO funds from outside into Eastern Europe and Russia. By not having fully recognized

[38] Open Society News, Fall 1995/Winter 1996, p. 9. Ironically the Open Society News
is published in New York City.

the need to develop the NPPO legal framework that will facilitate the in-flow of funds from the USA, the NPPO sector fostered by Soros will remain stunted. Neither the governments nor
the private sectors in Russian and Eastern Europe have the funding needed to substitute for and expand upon Soros' funding--funding limited by Soros' personal ability to maintain his pace.

Without the establishment of U.S.-Mexican type NPPO legislation that will permit foreign investors to establish company foundations, thus leaving some of their profits in Eastern Europe and Russia, then "nationalists" will be able to claim erroneously that their country is being sacked by greedy foreign capitalists.

Rather than creating competition, ironically Soros finds that he has to subsume it in order to save it, as in the case of Radio Free Europe. With the tremendous reduction in funds supplied by the USA, Radio Free Europe would not have survived had not in 1994 Soros moved it to Prague and reorganized it as part of his Open Media Research Institute (OMRI),[39] In this case Soros entered into a joint-venture to acquire Radio Free Europe's Research Institute and, under a fifty-year lease, its archives.[40]

---

[39] The OMRI Library contains archives Soros centered in Prague to save much of the communist history of Central and Eastern Europe and the former Soviet Union.

[40] Bruck ,"The World According to Soros," p. 71.

This paper analyzes the role of George Soros and the process of how he has assumed unique social leadership in the international philanthropic arena. He is a lone "global trouble-shooter" who, as of 1996, has donated half of his one-billion-dollar net worth to the Soros Foundation, which he has dedicated to help break statism in formerly Communist countries.

" With the breakthrough of the Internet to achieve instantaneous globalization, the Hungarian-born philanthropist has embarked on an ambitious plan to set up 30 Internet training centers across the far-flung regions of Russia [41] Bill Gates, whose business visit to Russia, just coincided with Soros', is just following into his footsteps.[42]

My approach in this chapter is to suggest the reason why Soros' noble attempt did not succeed in laying the basis for a broadly-financed and updated Marshal Plan for Eastern Europe. The goal of breaking up the statism that maintains the former Communist bloc countries as closed societies needs new NPPO laws that enable multi-track activity beyond the single-track offered by Soros. Soros funding of NPPO legal reform has encouraged only marginally countries to look outward. Ironically, he is leaving them on their own to look inward for lack of information about new trends in world philanthropy.

Soros' single-track efforts have involved creating branches of his Foundation in 25 countries of Eastern

42 Jeffrey, Williams, "In the Kremlin, a Computer Czar," *Los Angles Times, October 11, 1997, p. A11)*

Europe, Asia, and the Middle East by using U.S. NPPO law, not fostering the law itself as the legal basis needed for Western funders, including foreign investors who establish company foundations with some of the profits. Soros has yet to realize that the ideas he supports require a tax free and tax-deductible framework for the funding of community-based foundations that are able to make the thousands of decentralized decisions that he knows no central government can efficiently make.

To understand the Soros' initiative and its impact we must acknowledge the crisis of the modern welfare state in the USA as well as in Europe. The conviction has coalesced that overloaded and over bureaucratized government is incapable of performing the expanded task being assigned to it. The welfare state is the *incompetent* State.

In Eastern Europe the Incompetent State protected itself by use of totalitarian principles to maintain society closed to circulation of ideas and criticism of government. In Eastern Europe, as in the Russian Empire which was euphemistically called the "USSR," George Orwell's 1984 came true as the "democratic centralism" of Communist government destroyed the ability of communes to make any decisions for themselves.

Soros' Background And Career As Hedge-Fund Speculator

To establish a new type of "community interest" in Eastern Europe and Russia, George Soros determined in the 1980s to use his fortune to lead the way in establishing society open to the flow of information and criticism of government.

Soros had left Hungary for England in the 1947 to put behind him the experience of having lived under German and Russian occupations. He graduated from the London School of Economics in 1952; and he moved to the USA by 1956.[43] By the 1960s not only had he become an American citizen but was noted for his risk-taking investment practices especially in world financial markets, which brought him fortune as speculating in currency.

Since 1969 Soros has operated the Quantum Fund--a little-regulated,

---

[43] Connie Bruck, "The World According to Soros," The New Yorker, January 23, 1995, p. 59.

private-investment partnership based in Curacao (off the coast of Venezuela) geared to wealthy non-U.S. individuals, who typically attempt to achieve quick, outsized returns on highly leveraged "bets" that currency will appreciate or depreciate. His bets on currency culminated in his 1992 "breaking the Bank of England," which could not maintain the value of the pound in the face of the Soros-led speculation that England's currency was seriously over-inflated. [44]

Thirteen years before he won his six-billion bet against the pound sterling, Soros had begun to use his gains from speculation to support the opening of closed societies. He established in New

---

[44] George Soros and Byron Wien, <u>Soros on Soros: Staying Ahead of the Curve</u> (New York: John Wiley), 1995, pp. 81-83.

York the Open Society Fund in 1979, as an NPPO to support dissidents living under the Communist regimes, but he had kept a relatively low profile in doing so.

Soros--The Philanthropist

Indeed, Soros had been interested since his period in England to foster the democratic values of "an open society," as defined by the philosopher Sir Karl Popper.[45] Determined to make Popper's concept workable, Soros' Open Society Fund became the basis for the Open Society Fund, Inc. to which he has donated so much of his dubiously-earned profits to good ends.

[45] See Karl R., Popper The Open Society and Its Enemies, Princeton, New Jersey: Princeton University Press, 1995. Popper argues against the "closed society" of unquestioned authority advocated by Plato in The Republic.

Soros moved with high visibility into philanthropy by establishing in 1984 the Soros Foundation-Hungary and in 1987 the Soros Foundation-Soviet Union. After the fall of the Berlin Wall in 1989, Soros began to reposition himself by turning over the day-to-day management of his hedge fund to his staff so that he could immerse himself in the world of philanthropy. He was the only one who recognized and was able to do something about it that in those first moments after 1989 liberation from socialist dogma a new pattern of open society had to be set. His diagnosis was correct in that hardly had Russia and Eastern Europe overturned their dogmatic regimes that authoritarian forces attempted to seize power. This was hardly surprising because these had a complete absence of democratic experience and no modern political infrastructure was in place to support the new and fragile 'democracies.'

By 1990 he created three more foundations, moving into Central and Eastern Europe and the Soviet Union, dramatically accelerating the level of his giving. As Soros explains, "I have used financial markets as a laboratory for testing my theories... [on how to capitalize on] the collapse of the Soviet Empire."[46]

According to Soros' "Personal Statement" on the Soros Foundation World Wide Web Home Page, by early 1996 he was operating foundations in 24 countries. (The total is now 23, Belarus having this month withdrawn his legal recognition of Soros Foundation-Belarus, see below.)

[46] Soros on Soros, p. v.

Soros As Creator of Open Versus Closed Societies Via The Network

To change the course of history and prevent the return of centralized authoritarian power in Eastern Europe, Soros has attempted to build the framework needed to support democracy. Thus, he has established a large number of independent branch foundations that offer services and vehicles of self-expression outside the reaches of an increasingly discredited state. Since governments have neither the will nor the resources to lead the kinds of initiatives they once though that they could lead, Soros has been the leader in arguing that the vacuum of leadership should be filled by a socially responsible private sector. Therefore,

Soros has tried to set the philanthropic standard by opening branches of the Open Society Foundation around the globe.

Soros' views quoted below are taken from his oral interviews, speeches, books, articles, and foundation reports that provide the basis for his polyvalent concept 'open society,' as is seen for example in the 1994 Annual Report of the Soros Foundations:[47]

> The Soros is trying to make the family of Institutions independent by encouraging them to seek other sources of funding others than his own. As the Annual Report for the year 1994 puts it, "these organizations help build the infrastructure and institutions necessary for open

[47] P. 7.

societies by supporting a broad array of programs for education, children and youth, media and communications, civil society, human rights and humanitarian aid, science and medicine, arts, culture, and economic restructuring" Cit.

Telecommunications and the Internet have been the main tools in Soros' hand in his crusade for establishing the pattern of open societies. His prominent role in bringing down the Iron Curtain is indisputable.

The dramatic revolution and expansion in communications that took place during the 1980s, satellites, fax, copying machines, widespread dissemination of the computer opened the world's even most remote areas to the expanded communications links required for mass organization and concerted action contributed and accelerated the emergence of the fourth sector all around the world.

Analysis of Soros' use of the Internet shows how he uses electronic communication to influence other world leaders as well as how he uses the Net to unite the work worldwide of his foundations. Hence, he has initiated the Soros Foundation World Wide Web home page on the Internet.

George Soros has his own foreign policy. He has the money to back up his ideas and is spending it prodigiously. In 1994 alone, Soros' foundations around the world gave away $300 million, more than Portugal, New Zealand, or Ireland did, and he has spent a like amount in 1995. High-profile projects include a water purification plant in Sarajevo and a

$500 stipend for each of 30,000 Russian scientists.[48] For the Soros actual expenditures for 1994, see Tables 1 and 2.

Since 1990 he has devoted half of his income and a substantially large portion of his time and energy to developing his foundation network.[49]

In Soros' view, many Russians and Eastern Europeans are disillusioned and angry with the West, because the market economy being imported lacks a concept of common interest.[50] Soros agrees and notes that the U.S. model of

---

[48] Richard Teitelbaum, "What's Soros Up To Now?" Fortune, September 4, 1995,
   p. 94.

[49] Soros on Soros, p. 123.

[50] George Soros, "Address to the [Central European University] Budapest Graduation Ceremony," CEU Gazette, Spring/Summer 1995, p. 15.

untrammeled pursuit of self-interest does not represents the common interest. He argues that the U.S. model, which now dominates world development thinking, requires new rules and standards of behavior to circumscribe and contain competition, a measure of cooperation being needed to sustain competition.

The concept of open society is based on the recognition the world we live is inherently imperfect, as is human understanding of it, and although the U.S. model is morally corrupt, the great merit of its open society is to permit correction of faults. For Soros, the Western democracies are morally bankrupt if they subsume common interest to the pursuit of narrow self-interest. [51]

---

[51] Ibid.

Soros' goal is to turn the closed society of totalitarianism into an open society that follows Popper's prescription for setting "free the critical powers of man."[52] Before the revolutions that swept Central and Eastern Europe, dissidents had a similar goal; they called it "civil society," defined by some as" the connective tissue of democratic political culture." [53]

Soros credits his membership in the Helsinki Watch and Americas Watch human rights groups as sparking him his 1980 creation Open Society Fund to offer a number of scholarships in the United States to dissident intellectuals from Eastern Europe.[54] To credit that

---

[52] Popper The Open Society and Its Enemies, p.183.

[53] Soros "Address to the [Central European University] Budapest Graduation Ceremony," p. 15.

spark, he recruited Aryen Neyer, who was the head of Human Rights Watch, to become the president of Soros' Open Society Institute in New York City.

With the human-rights orientation of spreading information, one of Soros' first projects had been to offer photocopying machines to cultural and scientific institutions, which was the perfect way to undermine the Communist Party control of information in Hungary. As copying machines increasingly became available in 1984, the Party apparatus could not control the machines and the dissemination of information, thus, as Soros has stated, his foundation in Hungary enabled people who were not dissidents to act, in effect, like dissidents. Similarly, the Soros grant program for writers increased their

54 Soros on Soros, p. 115.

independence, therefore "disarming" the Party.[55]

Soros also tried to set up a foundation in China, establishing in 1986 the Fund for the Opening and Reform of China. That China operation was closed down by the Chinese government after the Tiananmen Square massacre, Soros being labeled as a "CIA agent."[56] Soros is optimistic about China, however, because with the rising number of fax machines and foreigners, it will be impossible to re-establish the rigid thought-control that prevailed previously.

To serve as "prototype" of open society, Soros' network of foundations has grown as follows: [57]

---

[55] The view above and below is drawn from Soros on Soros, 118-123.

[56] Ibid., 139.

[57] Soros Foundation, Internet Electronic

1984, Hungary

1986, China

1987, Russia

1988, Poland

1990, Bulgaria, Estonia,
Lithuania, Romania, and Ukraine 1991,
Yugoslavia

1992, Albania, Belarus, Bosnia
& Hercegovina, Croatia,
Czech Republic, Latvia,
Macedonia, Moldova, Slovenia

1993, Kazakhstan,
Kyrgyzstan, South Africa,

1994, Georgia

1995, Haiti, South Africa,
Burma

1997, Guatemala

According to Soros, these national
foundations are committed to certain

Communications, World Wide Web, "National Foundations," WWW.Soros.Org, March 1996.

common goals, such as the rule of a democratically elected government, a vigorous, diverse civil society, respect for minorities, and a free market economy. They also share a commitment to working together across national, ethnic, and religious boundaries to achieve these goals and such regional objectives as cooperation and peace among neighboring countries. The manner in which they pursue these goals is up to each national foundation, which, with its own staff and board, sets program priorities in response to the particular situation and problems in each country. These national foundations support, in part or in whole, a variety of internships abroad.

Recognizing the importance of incisive and responsible journalism, the Soros Foundations fund a broad array of activities to train and equip reporters, editors, and media managers for their new responsibilities in democratic, free market societies. The ultimate goal is to create an informed electorate that has access to diverse, objective are reports supplied by a press corps with high professional standards.

Foundations in Romania, Russia, and Ukraine have sent local journalists to CNN's U.S. headquarters in Atlanta, Georgia, for the six-week International Professional Program. Foundations in the former Yugoslavia sent reporters to London for two months of training and work at the Balkan War Report, the highly regarded publication of the Institute for War and Peace Reporting. The Soros foundations' priorities in the area of communications are support for the establishment of strong, independent media as well as the expansion of telecommunications throughout the above-mentioned regions.

Censorship in Central and Eastern Europe and the former Soviet Union is now less explicit than it was under communist regimes, who required that all broadcasts and newspapers pass through an official censor. Governments, however, still control much of the physical infrastructure of media transmission therefore exercising indirect censorship.[58]

Promptly, the National Foundations provided the print media have received access to international news services, desktop publishing equipment, electronic mail, printing presses, and even newsprint.

---

[58] New York Times Editorial: "The Not-So-Free Eastern European Press," October 2, 1995.

News outlets supported by national foundations include

Radijocentras, Lithuania;

Radio Vitosha, Bulgaria;

Uniplus, Romania;

Radio Tallin, Estonia;

Radio Echo of Moscow, Russia;

Feral Tribune, Croatia;

Ieve magazine, Ukraine;

Pritonmost, Czech Republic;

Vreme, Yugoslavia.

In Russia, the foundation is providing funds to refurbish more than two dozen independent radio stations and to organize them into a network for sharing information.

Soros-funded programs in Romania and Macedonia have acquired second-hand printing presses in the United States. The presses were refurbished and placed in independent printing houses. In supporting democratic movements, often times Soros is accused of meddling in internal affairs. For example, in Romania when the Soros Foundations faced in 1991 the government's attempt to quash news by increasing prohibitively the price of newsprint at election time, the Foundation bought newsprint abroad and trucks to import paper so that independent newspapers could continue to publish. President Iliescu subsequently accused Soros of supporting the opposition, to which Soros responded that he was only supporting a pluralistic, free press. [59]

In Romania, Soros has administered since 1994 the first public surveys ever taken and published them as the "Public Opinion Barometer." The

_____

[59] Soros on Soros, p. 139.

goal is to take the pulse of opinions about the country's economic and political life.

Soros is also founded in 1990 the Central European University (CEU) in Budapest, Prague, and Warsaw. The CEU is accredited in Hungary as degree-granting educational institution and prepares the leaders of the future. The CEU press publishing in English, Czech, Hungarian, Polish and Slovak languages provide news on the region in the domains of Literature, Political Science, Economics and European Studies.

Another fruitful program was established for the former Soviet and the Baltic states scientists, called the International Science Foundation. The scientists were given $100 million grant in order to continue their research in their native countries.[60] Emergency grants were given out of $500 to some 30,000 scientists, travel grants and scientific journals were provided, and the International Science Education Program is currently working to make the Internet available not only to the scientists but also to schools, universities, libraries and media.[61]

The Consortium for Academic Partnership, established in 1993, has expanded to include what Soros calls the "Virtual University," that is a program that includes:

---

[60] This and the following discussion is based upon Building Open Societies: Soros Foundations 1994, New York: OSI, 1994, pp. 15-35.

[61] World Wide Web. Soros Or. The International Science Foundation.

CEU scholarships for students to pursue doctoral work in the United States and Europe; professorial exchanges for the CEU Economics School; Freedom Support Act Fellowships; supplementary grants for students from the former Yugoslavia displaced by war; supplementary grants for Burmese students.

Support of education, either directly or as a component of other programs, is the main focus of Soros foundations activity, amounting to about 50% of the expenditures, according to Soros sources.

Education based on the values of open, pluralistic, democratic societies proved to be the most effective way to break the grip of the communist past and prevent the emergence of new closed societies based on nationalism.[62]

One of the most comprehensive educational programs of the Soros Foundation are the Transformation of the Humanities Project and the Social Science Projects, which attempt to undo the previously state-controlled educational system in Russia and the other countries of the former Soviet Union and ex-satellite states. The ambitious project to replace Marxist-Leninist text books and teaching in school and universities has been undertaken in cooperation with the Ministry of Education and commissioned thousands of books, training professors,

---

[62] This information on education and the following comes from ibid. and Building Open Societies, pp. 15-19.

giving grants to innovative schools, introducing new curricula at selected demonstration sites in various disciplines.[63]

The new textbooks, as well as Western texts adapted and translated for Russia, are being published at a rate of ten a month and 10,000 copies a run. The Transformation of Humanities Project has been replicated in Ukraine, Lithuania, Belarus, Estonia, Kazakhstan, Kyrgyzstan, Romania, Bosnia and Herzegovina, and Macedonia.

The Open Society Institute in Budapest conducts a number of research programs in collaboration with the CEU. Other foundations and programs created by George Soros include the International Science

---

[63] Soros on Soros , p.128.

Foundation (ISF) and the International Soros Science Education Program, both of which encourage and support scientists and science teachers in the former Soviet Union so that they will remain at work in their home countries and not sell their skills to weapons producers in areas such as the Middle East.[64]

Russia has been a difficult country for Soros. He began organizing the Soviet Cultural Initiative Foundation in 1987 only to have the management of it fall into the hands of a reformist clique of Communist Youth League officials, who paradoxically proceeded to form a closed society to promote an open one.[65]

[64] These programs are discussed, e.g., in the Annual Report of the Soros Foundations, 1994, and summarized on the Soros World Wide Web Internet pages.

[65] Ibid., p. 128.

For Soros, Gorbachev had the great merit to have first shaken the rigid power structure and break the isolation into which the Soviet Union had fallen. Gorbachev thought of Europe as an open society, where frontiers lose their significance. He envisaged Europe as a network of connections, not as a geographic location, the network extending the concept of civil society through an international arena. Such ideas could not be implemented by Gorbachev, but he must be credited with having planted them in infertile soil.[66]

In 1995, Soros reduced his financial investments in Russia, taking a "cautiously pessimistic' stance.[67] He is

---

[66] George Soros, <u>Opening the Soviet System</u> (London, Weidenfeld and Nicolson, 1990), p. 102.

[67] Michael, Gordon R., "Cautiously Pessimistic," but Investing in Russia <u>The New York Times</u>, December 22, 1995.

concerned that the xenophobic rhetoric by communists and nationalistic groups against greedy and exploitative foreigners is intended to provide an ideological justification for keeping the markets closed and protecting the resources for the state.[68] As Russia explodes out of the information vacuum that characterized the Communist era, the American magnate, financier-philanthropist is audaciously expanding access to the Internet and narrows the gap between Russia and the technologically advanced West.

Within his conception of open society, Soros sees the need for closer association between the nations of

---

[68] Michael, Gordon, R. "Russia's Woes Are Mirrored in the Decline of Coal Mines," New York Times, February 29, 1996.

Europe, provided that the state not define or dominate the international activities of the citizenry. His concept holds great appeal for people who have been deprived of the benefits of an open society. [69]

Soros' priority is to help give access to the world of information not only to journalists, as we have seen, but to other professional groups, especially including librarians and scientists as well as individual citizens. For Soros it is Electronic mail and Internet connectivity that hold the possibility of bringing to East-Central Europe and Russia a new method of communications particularly suitable to the building of open societies.[70]

---

[69] Soros, "Address to the [Central European University] Budapest Graduation Ceremony," p. 15.

[70] Open Society News, Fall 94, Electronic Edition, Soros Foundation (WWW.Soros.Org).

Making telecommunications widely available promotes pluralism and undermines government attempts to control information (Belarus has recently shut down the Open Society Foundation exactly for this reason). The Open Society foundations are building telecommunications networks by providing computers, software, training and the Internet access to media centers, libraries, legal institutes, research laboratories, high schools, universities as well as Soros foundation offices. Information servers are also being designed at a number of Soros organizations.

The hub of the Soros Foundations' communications activities is Open Media Research Institute, a new research center established to analyze and report on the political, economic, and social changes under way in Central and Eastern Europe and the former Soviet Union. It is developing a media studies program to teach journalists, analysts, policy specialists, and scholars about the role of investigative journalism as well as the business of media.[71]

What Soros desires, it would seem, is not only an open society, which might be an ideal one, but the creation of civic society--what the Romans called *civitas;* that is, public-spiritedness, sacrifice for the community, citizenship, especially elites. It involves the creation of what Francis Fukuyama calls "trust."[72]

In his oral interviews, Soros admits how difficult it is running a foundation in

---

[71] Idem, click on CEENet.Internet.

[72] Francis, Fukuyama, Trust: Social Virtues and the Creation of Prosperity, (New York: The Free Press, 1995), p. 27.

a revolutionary environment of Russia and the Eastern European countries. Despite a bitter 1994 experience of attempting to operate a foundation at the height of Russia's period of "robber-capitalists," Soros sees his Transformation of the Humanities Project as very successful.[73]

To provide students with information on educational opportunities in the West, 23 Soros Student Advising Centers have been established in major cities in the Eastern European region. The foundations also promote the English language through a variety of local projects.[74]

---

[73] Soros on Soros, passim, esp. p. 129.

[74] International Guide to Funders Interested in Central and Eastern Europe Central European Foundation Center (EFC), Brussels, Belgium, 1993, p. 147.

Responding to the unique intellectual and emotional needs of children and teens, the Open Society Institute has initiated a series of regional programs to provide opportunities for the young people in the region and especially in the countries of former Yugoslavia.

At the time when a changing political landscape offers little stability, the Regional High School Debate Program and the Preschool Project promote independence and self-esteem, and encourage young people to take an active and critical role in their education.[75] Most national foundations contribute project support to indigenous, independent organizations which

---

[75] Chris, Sulavek, "Empowering the Programs for Children and Teens,"
Open Society News, Winter 1995, p. 5.

address cultural, major health or environmental problems in direct and practical ways: fellowships sending American volunteers abroad to teach environmental topics, donating medical supplies, distribution networks, and dollar conversion for the purchase of desired medical equipment.[76]

With regard to philanthropy for medical goals, Soros' concern about the problem in the USA caused him to initiate a "Project on Death and Dying," dedicated to research and issues of terminal illness and pain management, on which he intends to focus more of his energies and funds. The goal of the Soros Project on Death in America is to help expand our understanding of and to transform the forces that have created

---

[76] International Guide to Funders Interested in Central and Eastern Europe, p. 147.

and sustain the current culture of dying. The $5,000 million project supports epidemiological, ethnographic, and historical research and other programs that illuminate the social and medical context of dying and grieving.[77] In Soros' own words the American medical culture, "modern medicine is so intent on prolonging life that it fails to prepare us for death." The results of the research will help to encourage family involvement and to reduce the dehumanizing effect of medical treatment. Under the Grants Program, Joseph's House in Washington, DC, a Project on Death on America grantee, provides a life-affirming community for people with AIDS.

---

[77] George, Soros "Reflections on Death in America," Open Society News, Winter 1995, p. 2.

Soros' foundations herald an era in which social and cultural responsibility, assumed by government up to the 1980s in Eastern Europe, is defined by private giving. Soros Foundation grants to Eastern Europe outstrip the amounts given by most Western corporate foundations in Europe. Soros' funding has gone less to construct capitalism than to rediscover the human riches of intellect that communism plundered.

In its focus on finance and government, the West has neglected the softer and subtler sides of free societies, and Soros' new Marshal plan (1989) was "greeted with amusement" by the Europeans. [78]

---

[78] Barry, Newman, "Soros Gives to Help East Europe Recover Lost Cultural Treasures," New York Times, March 22, 1994.

With regard to failure of policies he has supported, Soros notes with regret that the Russian programs partially failed because of his leaders there bought autos for their personal use. Therefore, he temporarily closed operations in order to organize an entirely new staff. The foundations involved in structural reforms in Ukraine, and Macedonia, the last surviving multi-ethnic democracy have been successful. The $50 million granted to the young Macedonian state just saved it from bankruptcy. (L'Evenement, No. 583, p.27)

In late February the Milosevic regime in Belgrade (Serbia) dealt a financial blow to Soros programs in two ways. It hurt all independent media by revoking the registration of the Soros Foundation, forcing it to close down operations in Serbia and Montenegro.

This also has slowed the work of the Open Society Institute work in Belgrade where it is developing an important part of its A Balkan War Crimes Database.[79]

The Soros Foundation Model Unfollowed

Why has Soros won neither foundations or multilateral agencies to "invest" as he has in the development of post-communist society?

The answer has several parts. First, Soros has been concerned that his Foundations not become the kind of bureaucratic operation run by a meritocratic elite for itself (thus requiring long lead time to develop projects) that has taken power in most foundations and all multilateral development banks and agencies. Second, as a

---

[79] New York Times Editorial: "Censorship in the Balkans," March, 14, 1996.

consequence of the first point, Soros has been able to do what most foundations cannot do not only because his entire financial trading history is based upon that of being a risk-taker who grasps the moment. Because most foundation leaders and all leaders of multilateral development and banking agency are risk averse, too often they miss the opportunity to be a part of genuinely new programs.   To make grants without incurring total accounting responsibility over expenditures by the grantee, U.S. and U.S.-based multilateral banks and agencies must make pay their lawyers to make a legal determination that each grantee is the "equivalent to a U.S. NPPO" and if it would be eligible for certification by the IRS if it were a U.S. NPPO.

Soros' solution to the above legal problem is to have set up his own network of foundations that at once facilitates his grant making activity and gives them some independence, yet allows him to provide a check on expenditure should he not make new grants.

What happens when Soros runs out of money and/or dies? What has he institutionalized? The answers do not bode well for the future of the NPPO sector for which he hopes his foundations are the model for others to follow:

The problem is that without a NPPO legal framework to encourage internationally-oriented foundation "investment" in Eastern Europe, the Soros Foundation Model cannot easily be followed, leaving Soros to stand alone as the funder of only resort. The challenge to Soros is not to be the sole funder in each country because the task of establishing the open basis for civil society requires the spending of billions of dollars by funders making the thousands of decisions no one organization can make. Beyond Soros' use of funds to support debate and spread of information, Soros must now help support the NPPO legal basis for the establishment of competing foundations. Without competition, Soros Foundation decisions about whom to fund have the political consequence of alienating those who are not funded and who are without other recourse as the State contracts.

Yet Soros' Open Society Institute, which itself is funded from the USA, determined at a 1995 meeting of the

East Program, that "international funding is not the solution for the long-term future" of the NPPO sector in Russia and Eastern Europe. Hence, the meeting concluded that it should look inward to develop private funding sources in each country of the region.[80]

The East meeting not only runs counter to Soros' own experience of encouraging the flow of NPPO funds from outside into Eastern Europe and Russia. By not having fully recognized the need to develop the NPPO legal framework that will facilitate the in-flow of funds from the USA, the NPPO sector fostered by Soros will remain stunted. Neither the governments nor the private sectors in Russian and Eastern Europe

---

[80] Open Society News, Fall 1995/Winter 1996, p. 9. Ironically the Open Society News is published in New York City.

have the funding needed to substitute for and expand upon Soros' funding-- funding limited by Soros' personal ability to maintain his pace.

Without the establishment of U.S.-Mexican type NPPO legislation that will permit foreign investors to establish company foundations, thus leaving some of their profits in Eastern Europe and Russia, then "nationalists" will be able to claim erroneously that their country is being sacked by greedy foreign capitalists.

Rather than creating competition, ironically Soros finds that he has to subsume it in order to save it, as in the case of Radio Free Europe. With the tremendous reduction in funds supplied by the USA, Radio Free Europe would not have survived had not in 1994 Soros moved it to Prague and reorganized it as part of his Open Media Research Institute (OMRI),[81] In this case Soros entered into a joint-venture to acquire Radio Free Europe's Research Institute and, under a fifty-year lease, its archives.[82]

CONCLUSION

Granted Soros' many "successes" outlined in this study, the sheer number of activities over which Soros has taken personal responsibility and active on-going interest is simply incredible. Soros has done so with little central bureaucracy in New York City by recessing thousands of persons to

---

[81] The OMRI Library contains archives Soros centered in Prague to save much of the communist history of Central and Eastern Europe and the former Soviet Union.

[82] Bruck ,"The World According to Soros," p. 71.

whom the development of national programs has been delegated.

Although Soros has not led foundations to follow him into Eastern Europe and Russia, in the long term his foundations provide a model for the future, a model that works without regard to borders.[83] Regardless of what his detractors claim, he has put his profits to good use. The paradoxes of my analysis are as follows:

Soros has opened a healthy competition by engaging in the "race of giving" with Ted Turner (owner of CNN) and Bill Gates (Micrososft.) This triangle has creator a real healthy competition in giving, mark of an internationalization of the community spirit. In Latin America,

[83] Williams, Carol, J. "In the Kremlin, a Computer Czar," Los Angles Times, October 11, 1997, p 7

99

Soros is spearheading a human rights and social activist program to improve education and open communications in Guatemala.[84]

As a responsible capitalist, Soros helps building democracy into the communities across nations by implicitly replicating the U.S. model of NGO that consists of: an open elected board made up of "all-walks-of-life", that means of local prestigious people from different interest groups; businessmen, doctors, academics, union leaders etc.

Projects are being funded by open review of the projects and there is transparency in the expenditure (foundations have to submit a final report at the end of the year). If the NGOs have not been successful in completing the

[84] Poole Claire, "A New Latin Empire" Latin Trade, November 1997, p. 35

operation, no further funding will be available.

So, for those claiming his foundations are not democratic, let us compare it with The Red Cross (foundation that is indeed undemocratic, by being headed by a self-selecting board.)

About Soros with a foreign board of directors, leaves them with the decision to prioritize at local level and fund the projects most timely.

As Mahateer suggests of Soros being a "speculator," we have to mention here that investment is also a kind of speculation: sometimes one loses, sometimes one wins; and hedge-funds are meant for that (he lost big in Mexico in 1994 speculating against the peso). Rather than admitting defeat, Soros has invested in real estate, he inked a joint venture to develop three ambitious projects in Mexico City: Alameda Urbana, Santa Fe and, the tallest building in the country, the Chapultepec Tower.

Althought, some observers have seen Soros as one who "colonizes" needy countries as a benevolent despot[85], networking would be a better word. Neither was he offering "a new type of American imperialism" to the world, in reality he made high risk investments, that he finally ran out of his legendary good fortune as Soros wanted to keep his money up so that he could support his foundations that were eating up at

---

[85] Contends Professor Geoffrey Symcox (UCLA), attacking Soros at the Colloquium on European History in October 1997, on the grounds that Soros is not an investor.
Actually Soros is the biggest landowner in Argentina and Russia. He has recently set up other five NPPOs in Guatemala

his portofolio so he decided to retreat from bad investments.

Focusing more on his philanthropic funds and taking high risks, Soros lost 22% of his portofolio.[86] Markets now are too complex, he pointed out, to make a huge fund work, "the bigger it got [the firm] the more difficult it became, Mr. Soros said."[87] Rather than riling the financial markets, after a bet on technology funds had left the fund down 22%, Soros had decided to do less risky investments, and will invest in "more conservative real-estate and private-equity funds."[88]

---

[86] Alan Cowell, "Soros reveals Plan For Quantum Fund," The New York Times, June 16, 2000

[87] Gregory Zuckerman, "George Soros Alters His Style Making A Role For His Son Robert,"
The Wall Street Journal, June 16, 2000

[88] Ibid., p.C11

And watch for market swings. That combined with the bad investments in Russian telecommunication systems cost him dearly.

His indisputable merit is that of replicating the American model of NGOs and leaving behind a legacy of philanthropic "incubators."
Against the open society, its enemies have proliferated: they are not only the "classic" ideologies (fascism, marxism or nationalism) but also the successful ideologies like laissez-faire, radical liberalism, geopolitical realism and social darwinism.[89]

To conclude, when Soros started out in hedge-funds, there was no

---

[89] Dan Suciu, "George Soros –The Man Who Wants To Change the World," Lumea, No. 4, Bucharest, 2000

competition. And now competition is so fierce, as all his moves are being

observed.
And Soros fell in his own "trap", as the markets he once moved to his benefit, are moving against him, to his detriment after the disastrous financial collapse in 2008 in the United States.

Enemies of the nation

Cécile Tormay, a Hungarian author has written much about Soros, and accuses

him of being the enemy of the Nation, just like in 1984, in the novel by George Orwell, Goldstein was considered fomenting anarchy and ethnic strife. A mastermind with a masterplan for global domination.

Prime Minister Orbán's and the far right had completely neglected the

Hungarian people's needs.

 He conveniently forgets the multiple failures of the Fidesz government party, a Dictatorial monopolistic party he heads since 2010, Orbán has triumphantly ignored all international regulations.

And systematically succeeded in eroding democracy and the rule of law, as noted by Jan-Werner Müller, Matthijs Bogaards and numerous other academics.

The anti-George Soros campaign is being financed by tax payers money, had been intensified by FIDESZ to discredit the mogul, and obtain support from the hateful Hungarians for reelection. No young Hungarian would believe his accusations; they would rather emigrate to other countries

where there are real opportunities to get ahead.

However, Orbán has failed to significantly improve living standards, healthcare,

and education in Hungary in the past years, and uses anti-semitic propaganda to

get re-elected.[90]

Russia, and Romania have also banned and closed down his organizations.

For me, this is a sign that the specter of communism is back in all Eastern

European countries.

Regardless of what his detractors claim, he has put his profits to good
use.

---

[90] Read Cecile Tormay, and *Protocols of the Elders of Zion*.

In conclusion, the paradoxes of my analysis are as follows:

Soros has opened a healthy competition by engaging in the "race of giving" with Ted Turner (owner of CNN) and Bill Gates (Micrososft.) This triangle has created a real healthy competition in giving, mark of an internationalization of the giving to the community spirit. Furthermore, In Latin America, Soros is spearheading a human rights and social activist program to improve education and open communications in

Guatemala.

As a responsible capitalist, Soros

helps building democracy into the

communities across nations by implicitly

replicating the U.S. model of NGO that

consists of: an open elected board made

up of "all-walks-of-life", namely that

means of local prestigious people from

different interest groups; businessmen,

doctors, academics, union leaders etc.

Projects are being funded by open

review of the projects and there is

transparency in the expenditure

(foundations have to submit a final report

at the end of the year). If the NGOs have

not been successful in completing the

operation, no further funding will be

available.

So, for those claiming his foundations

are not democratic, let us compare it

with The Red Cross (foundation that is

indeed undemocratic, by being headed

by a self-selecting board.)

About Soros's innovation, as he

insists all these organizations have a

foreign (that is local) board of directors, leaves them with the decision to prioritize at local level and fund the projects most timely.

As Mahateer suggests of Soros being a "speculator," we have to mention here that investment is also a kind of speculation: sometimes one loses, sometimes one wins; and hedge-funds are meant for that (he lost big in Mexico in 1994 speculating against the peso). Rather than admitting defeat, Soros has invested in real estate, he inked a joint venture to develop three ambitious projects in Mexico City: Alameda Urbana, Santa Fe and, the tallest building in the country, the Chapultepec Tower.

Although some observers have seen Soros as one who "colonizes" needy countries as a benevolent despot47, networking would be a better word. Neither was he offering "a new type of American imperialism" to the world, in reality he made high risk investments, that he finally ran out of his legendary good fortune as Soros wanted to keep

his money up so that he could support

his foundations that were eating up at

his portofolio so he decided to retreat

from bad investments.

Focusing more on his philanthropic

funds and taking high risks, Soros lost

22% of his portofolio.48

 Markets now are too complex, he

pointed out, to make a huge fund work,

"the bigger it got [the firm] the more

difficult it became, Mr. Soros said."49

Rather than riling the financial markets,

after a bet on technology funds had left

the fund down 22%, Soros had decided

to do less risky investments, and will

invest in "more conservative real-estate

and private-equity funds."50

And watch for market swings. That

combined with the bad investments in

Russian telecommunication systems

cost him dearly.

His indisputable merit is that of

replicating the American model of NGOs

and leaving behind a legacy of

philanthropic "incubators."

Against the open society, its enemies have proliferated: they are not only the "classic" ideologies (fascism, marxism or nationalism) but also the successful ideologies like laissez-faire, radical liberalism, geopolitical realism and social darwinism.51

To conclude, when Soros started out in hedge-funds, there was no competition. And now competition is so fierce, as all his moves are being observed in Europe as well as in the United States.

And Soros fell in his own "trap", as the

markets he once moved to his benefit,

are moving against him, to his detriment.

One recent brilliant initiative has been

taken By Blockchain technology together

with Soros, are working on putting

asylum seekers money up on

Blockchain. This move will protect the

emigrants and immigrants in their quest

for a country. The refugee's money will

be protected, and they will have money

available to see a doctor, buy food, and

or to settle in the host country. This pot

of money can be accessed by the

refugees themselves or the host-

government in the event of sanitation, or

nutritional needs of the migrants, or

asylum seekers.

And all this because Hungary had been

so unhappy with the Muslim immigrants,

who were literally thrown out of the

country in 2017.

Thank you for reading my book.

If you like this, more Books on Kindle:

1. Dr Olga's Dream Come True
2. Decentralized Globalization: Free Trade and Civic Engagement And Civil Society.
3. Decentralized Globalization.

Olga Lazin at UCLA, January 15, 2018

Made in the USA
Las Vegas, NV
04 March 2022

44985954R00066